Overcoming the Past to Create a
More Powerful, Beautiful, Mindful You!

Brenda Colter

Copyright © 2019 Brenda Colter

All rights reserved. No part of this publication may be reproduced, distributed, or transmitted in any form or by any means, including photocopying, recording, or other electronic or mechanical methods, without the prior written permission of the Publisher, except in the case of brief quotations embodied in critical reviews and certain other noncommercial uses permitted by copyright law. For permission requests, write to the author, addressed "Attention: Permissions Coordinator," at the address below.

Brenda Colter

Herbeautifulmind220@gmail.com

www.Herbeautifulmind220.com

Publishing Coordination & Cover Design By

ThriveHer Publishing House visit us at
www.rrebirthingcenter.com

All rights reserved.

Dedication

This book is dedicated to the woman who feels misunderstood. To the woman who is sick and tired of being sick and tired and is now ready to walk in the ordained greatness that God has set aside just for her. This book is for the woman who spends her days engulfed in a facade of composure but under the cloak of darkness, at night, in her most secret heart of hearts, she feels broken and afraid.

This book is for you. It will be for you like nothing or no one else has ever been before. I dedicate this book to you with assurance that you can free yourself from it all with the tools herein... just as I did.

Contents

Dedication iii
Acknowledgments vii
Introduction ix
1. Shed, Release, Grow 1
2. Serving 'Self' On A Platter 11
3. Who's Driving Your Car? 27
4. Transforming Experiences 37
5. Building Realistic Relationships 53
6. Positive Energy = Powerful you 69
About The Author 79

Acknowledgments

I absolutely have to begin by thanking God... for so many different reasons. I thank God for His patience, His grace, His mercy, His peace and most of all His love. During the times that I have felt the most unlovable, it's brought comfort to know that God has been there by my side, guiding me every step of the way. To my mother and my father (God rest his soul), thank you for giving me the best parts of each of you. To my children, thank you for your unconditional love. I've never been perfect and yet you all give me your perfect love and that love has been a guidepost leading me through some of my darkest days. Brandon, thank you for being my best friend and for forgiving me for missing the mark on being anything resembling a perfect mother. You've been my rock from the moment I laid eyes on you. You are my Zion. Marzjae' thank you for your brutal honesty and your protection of me. You keep me on my toes and won't allow me to accept anything other than what I deserve, and in your eyes I deserve the very best. Cazjmere, thank you for mothering me when I miss the mother mark. You take care of our family when I'm working and never complain... that's a lie, you complain all of the time but you never let that stop you. Your belief in my abilities and sharing my goals has been the reason that I continue on this grind. Corey, thank you for challenging my thoughts. You are the most strong-willed person that I know and one of the few people left on this plant with a genuinely good heart. I see the light of the world in your eyes and you make me know that there is a reason for my being. Kat, who would have thought that the most caring HR Manager that I've ever known, through the countless times that you had to save my job, would ever be my business partner and best friend? And the best one on the planet might I add. Thank you for trusting and believing in me when I had a hard time doing it myself. To all of my friends, family and clients, thank y'all for the experiences and lessons. It's way too many of y'all to name individually but just know that I love every single one of you and appreciate all that you have done during the course of my life to aid me in becoming the woman that I am today. All of y'all will get individual thanks in the memoir though because all of y'all will be in it! Ha! Thank you to Coach Robyn and the RRE team! This would not be possible without you. Your guidance, direction and coaching has been invaluable!

I felt caught off guard and just plain old stuck. I had practiced for my very first interview for weeks and the time was finally here. During the interview, I was concise, clear, straight to the point and feeling like I was sitting on top of the world until the interviewer threw me a curveball. I had been sent over questions in advance, so that I would be prepared, but here she was, asking me a question that was NOT on my sheet. A question that unbeknownst to me would be the catalyst to my decision of whether or not to write this book. But first, I had to answer her. On the fly. With no practice. For someone in my filed, this question should have been easy to answer. After all, I have worked with plenty of women and brought each of them to the place where they could address this very concern. My mouth went dry, my pause felt like it lasted an eternity. How forthcoming should I be? Was now the time? Should the world know my story? Was I ready to give my testimony? It was here, in my very first interview that I began to bare my soul.

Before I get into the details of my response, I should probably offer a little background about who I am and why it's important. My name is Brenda Colter and I am an Emotional Wellness Coach. What does that mean? It means that I coach and mentor women and young girls on how to increase the peace in their lives, which is achieved by simply teaching them how to STEER their way towards peace, passion and purpose. If you take nothing else from this book it should be that we need to learn how to preserve energy by accepting people, places and things for who they are, how they are, when they are. The best way to create said peace, is to retrain the brain to a more productive mindset. I utilize a proprietary program called STEER which I will go more into later. For now it's enough to know that very few of us realize that this seemingly simple concept can be the difference between calm and chaos in our lives, and for those of us who do know; there is still the matter of how to do it that escapes us. My life's work is to teach the how.

Knowing where my expertise lies will now help you to understand why there is probably no reason that I should have been so stumped by the interviewer's question. Now looking back on it, I completely understand what was happening. I was on the precipice of purpose. In this moment, my destiny was being written by my answer. Okay, okay, okay... I'm getting on with it. The question that the interviewer asked was:

"Brenda, with all the clients you've helped, is there any common roadblock that most people seem to be dealing with?"

After all of the drama of the emotions that I felt above, my response flowed fluently:

"The past." I said with confidence, "I find that most people do exactly as I did early on in life. They never deal with the issues of their past and eventually just become resigned to the pain and become almost complacent in it. They take on a kind of 'it is what it is' mentality and don't understand that these issues can be resolved by allowing time to reprocess the thoughts that are attached to them and seek resolve."

Here I took a breath. A very deep one. I had survived and she should be getting back to the script now, right? Wrong! No such luck.

She went on, "Why is it so important to resolve our challenges deriving from our past?"

After the briefest of pauses, I responded, "Well, we've discussed how a thought is just a sentence in our minds, and beliefs are thoughts that we think over and over. Where the past is concerned, this means that we have believed this for so long our brains are wired to think about these things whether we want to or not. It's become ingratiated into who we are. So either we can keep thinking about them in the way that we always have which breeds pain and discontentment. Or we can rethink the situations in a more productive manner that encourages wisdom and growth. Combining the practical process that I teach with prayer and meditation shows that there doesn't have to be this vast chasm between stagnation and progress. We can shorten the distance and make the leap from the former to the latter."

The moment I completed the statement, I knew what I had to do. I had to get this message to the world and offer some tips and tricks to overcoming the past. I am going to show you that there is a practical way to leave the past in the past by offering you an introduction into a self-coaching model that I teach and how to apply it to everyday life. Now that we have an understanding of what drives me, how about we delve into what made you purchase the book. To begin, I just would like for you to take a moment now and think about your past. Think of some things from your past that are still effecting you negatively today. Take some time and write those things down.

Brenda Colter

HER Beautiful Mind

"If you are depressed you are living in the past. If you are anxious you are living in the future. If you are at peace you are living in the present."

~ Lao Tzu

1

Shed, Release, Grow

Upon completion of the interview, I began to think about my clients and my own life's journey. What were some other themes that I noticed? It was in that moment I realized that most of us struggle with time in general. Just like the past can take us up and essentially hold us hostage, worrying about the future can consume us and keep us in an ever-present state of anxiety. Now this is not an admonition against planning, preparing or wanting to attempt some semblance of structure. I am speaking of the worry, concern and being debilitatingly consumed with what's to come. The worry that keeps us up at night and can cause nightmares and panic attacks.

Fairly early on in my life, I was plagued with panic attacks, or anxiety attacks as they are also called. When I began my healing process, it became necessary for me to assess and analyze the source of my attacks which was when I noticed the pattern. The manifestation of my frustrations was typically a direct result of worrying. Worrying about the direction of my life. Worrying about what tomorrow would bring. Worrying about whether I would get my life in order in enough time to be of any use to my children. Worrying about how I would ultimately place myself in a position to win, and what did that even look like? Have you ever experienced a panic attack? They actually can manifest in a myriad of ways which is totally contingent upon the person who is in the throes of anxiety. For me, I would feel like I was on the brink of death.

I can still remember most of my attacks as though they were yesterday. The most notable one occurred when I thought my life was over. I was 14 years old and sitting in Planned Parenthood. Something wasn't right inside. I couldn't explain it. I was sick all of the time and so very tired. The birth control pills that I had been taking with no one besides my best friend's knowledge had stopped my monthly period and the symptoms went right with it. So what was wrong with me? My girl kept me calm as we waited but I still jumped visibly when the receptionist called my name. They allowed to her come to the back room with me and the doctor began.

"Well young lady... you are pregnant." I looked at my friend, she looked back at me. We had been friends long enough to know what was running through both of our minds. I'm going to die... I'm going to literally die because my mother will kill me. Here I was, Miss Straight-A-Goody-Two-Shoes, pregnant at 14. I couldn't think so my friend rattled off the questions as I sat in shock. The doctor answered her questions but her eyes never left me. They both sounded so far away. I heard her ask the doctor:

"So how did this happen if she is on the pill?" The doctor replied,

"Well the pill is only 99.9% effective so there is that very small percentage. There could be a variation of instances that could cause the pill to fail." She then turned to me. "Have you recently began taking any antibiotics at all? Any antifungal medications? I don't see a history of seizures or sleep disorders in your chart, but is there something you could be forgetting?"

My bestie responded for me, "No. She doesn't have any of that."

The doctor continued, "Well whatever the root cause, this is indeed something that will need to be discussed with your parents..."

At the word "parents" my brain went ballistic. What was going to happen to me? What had I done to my future? How could I go to college with a baby? How would I finish high school? Where would I live? Would I keep the baby? Would it be a good person? How could I raise a child when I was still a child myself? What if something was wrong with it? What if I died in childbirth because I was so young? Would my mother make me have an abortion? Did I want to have an abortion? What would my father say? Will everyone hate me? Was I going to hell? Had I disappointed God? Why didn't I consider all of this before? These questions hit me like a blast from a shotgun with each one creating damage to my psyche. One by one they reverberated through me with the intensity of a buckshot.

It began as a lump in my throat that I had difficulty swallowing over. The attempts to swallow soon affected my ability to breathe. I felt as though no matter how deeply I breathed in, I couldn't get enough air. I began to hyperventilate so intensely that my chest felt as though it would explode. I just knew that if this went on long enough I would eventually lose consciousness. I was getting dizzy and everyone was rushing around me. The next thing I knew, I was waking up on the gurney with an oxygen mask covering my face. This was my first panic attack, but it wouldn't be my last.

In that moment, I developed a habit that would follow me for years to come. I would endure worrying and suffering behind matters that either I couldn't change or matters that could be thought out with strategic planning and possibly even end up in my favor. Worrying about the future only consumes brain power that could be used more practically. That's what retraining your brain is all about. Relearning the developed patterns from our past experiences to create more helpful and productive ways of thinking.

Do you ever find yourself absolutely consumed by thoughts about your future? What are some things that you can do to quiet those concerns? Do you ever find yourself feeling down or depressed? What can you do to ultimately overcome those feelings?

HER Beautiful Mind

Brenda Colter

So how does one stay engaged in the present and ensure that we are equally and properly managing our time, thoughts and emotions? We learn. We study. We grow. We cultivate appreciation and acceptance. We do these things in consideration of not just ourselves, but others as well. Most of us don't realize that there are often insecurities attached to the decisions that we make and also the ones that we refuse to make. This means that the first step is to shed the insecurities. Which is notably more easily said than done, but the good news is that it's possible.

We have to learn that as long as we accept ourselves, most of our insecurities, concerns and present day issues can be cleared away by vanquishing the desire to be accepted by others. Frequently we find ourselves being concerned about the outcome of situations based upon how it might look in the eyes of others or what others may think. Realizing that most people have already formed an opinion of what they believe to be true about you and will likely twist any situation to fit inside their preconceived frame of mind will decrease the likelihood of your being concerned with their perceptions. This concept will come full circle in the next chapter when we discuss self-acceptance and the knowledge of self. When we know and love who we are, the opinions of others are not just secondary, they become nonexistent.

Another major step in the pursuit of growth is to identify in this moment, what needs to be done to achieve our desired outcomes in life. On occasion, we need to do a quick cursory examination regarding whether or not the choices and decisions we are making exemplify who we want to recognize ourselves as in this world. Ask yourself, 'Does this choice honor me?', 'Does this decision exemplify who I want to be in Christ?', or 'In the interest of universal influence, does this place me in a position to win?.' Being able to answer these questions in a way that makes us proud is key to ensuring constant elevation.

Think about some things in your life that you need to shed or release? Who do you ultimately want to grow to be in life? Write about it.

Brenda Colter

HER Beautiful Mind

"It's self-FULL to put yourself first; to be as good as possible to you, to take care of you, to keep you whole and healthy."

~ Iyanla Vanzant

2

Serving 'Self' On A Platter

Who are you? Do you know yourself? Do you love yourself. Do you even like yourself? For a long time I absolutely did not have the answers to any of these questions. Having what I considered to be a detached mother, a borderline absentee father and being sexually assaulted by a trusted family friend at a very young age created a cynicism in me that wasn't easily quelled. I believed that if the two people who brought me into this world didn't care for me, no one else would either. I grew to believe that love was fictitious and that included self-love. In my heart of hearts, I believed that complacency was all that a person could hope for. Happiness was simply a myth.

What was always so ironic about me was the fact that my low self-esteem did not manifest the way that most others did. When one identifies a textbook case of self-esteem issues, we typically find words like withdrawn, quiet, sullen. With me it was more boisterous, defiant and even violent at times. I thought that developing a sense of acceptance was the same as esteem and that through that acceptance, I was empowering myself. I became complacent and content in the fact that I just wasn't that pretty and probably never would be, I also felt that I had an excuse to be bitter and angry so if I accepted it, others would have to as well or simply keep it moving.

I now know that what I was doing was creating a defense mechanism. I drew a line between myself and others that effectively created a battleground for communications and interactions. My solution to all of this was to strike before anyone else could. All of this occurred in the name of self-love as far as my warped mind could comprehend. My logic was that I clearly loved myself, because if I didn't, I wouldn't be trying so hard to protect myself. This all became disturbingly clear one day during a conversation with a friend. We were discussing a party that we were going to and what we would wear.

"You should wear that one red top that you have, with the black pants and the knee high boots. I love that outfit on you and you look really good in red" she told me.

I responded, "Nah, I was thinking about wearing the short skirt with the semi-crop and my black brass knuckle heals."

"Oh, well yeah... you could wear that too. I like the other one better though. I think I might wear...."

My brain shut off. To this day, I don't know what she said during the rest of the conversation. I had no clue what she said that she was wearing. I was too busy processing the shade that I had perceived. *Was she saying that I didn't look cute in the outfit that I wanted to wear? Oh I know, because my legs are so big, she doesn't think I should wear short skirts. And the crop isn't a 'CROP, crop,' it's just a little shorter in the front, but I'm sure she's thinking that I shouldn't show my stomach. And those are my favorite shoes so they would be a little scuffed. They weren't going to stay perfect forever, but they weren't that bad and I can't help that I can't afford any new ones.* All of this happened in a matter of mere moments. So I did what I knew best. I engaged my defense mechanism and just let each of these thoughts flow out of my mouth just in case it was what she was thinking. Let me remind you that she had given no indication that she felt this way. This inner dialogue was mine and mine alone. Before I knew it, an entire self-deprecating diatribe fell out of my mouth as if she had spoken my thoughts.

When I finished she just looked at me as if I was an alien who had just landed on earth. Utter confusion spread across her face as she asked me, "Why do you do that?

"Do what?" I asked.

"You always say such negative things about yourself and it usually doesn't bother me, but I always wonder why someone would say such horrible things about themselves" I instantly burst into tears.

It had become second nature for me and I never even thought about why I did it, but when she asked me about it I felt like I had gotten hit with a ton of bricks.

"I just figured I would be honest before anyone else could use it against me." I answered.

"But honest by whose standards?" was her question, and since I had no answer, that shut the topic down. We went on to plan our evening and never spoke of the conversation again, but it stayed with me. I thought about the exchange and decided that it was time to take an internal gander at my thought processes and find out exactly how I felt about myself. How did I think about myself? Should it matter how others saw me? Did I even see myself at all?

I began with the physical. I simply stood stark naked into a full length mirror and instead of identifying my flaws, I began to search for beauty. Each occurrence of beauty that I found, I wrote down. Head to toe, I explored my physicality and actually found some notable intricacies that made me feel beautiful. I then considered by behavior, speech and demeanor. What was the intention behind some of the things that I said? What was my desired outcome? In that moment, I was determined for my self-analysis to propel me into becoming the woman that I was destined to be. I didn't know her yet, but I was determined to get to know her. My elevation to true self-love proved to be an emotional excursion through identifying, probing and working to change the thought processes that created the monster that I had become. I became determined to love myself so that I could love others in the way that God intended. It was during this time that I began to understand how the wall that I had built was not just a boundary which can be quite helpful as long as it's healthy, but it had become a blockade not to be penetrated by anyone. This was why I was so alone. I had ostensibly shut everyone out.

  Have you considered whether you exemplify self-love? Is it true to your core, or is it a facade that you use to keep others at bay? If your self-love is genuine, what are some steps that you took in order to build it to the point that it is at today? If you haven't learned to practice self-love yet, what do you think that you need to do in order to come to a point where you love yourself above all else?

HER Beautiful Mind

While I would love to say that the conversation that I had with my friend changed my life and I lived happily ever after, that's just not how life works. I'm really convinced that it isn't the way that life is even supposed to work. When I consider all that I have learned and ultimately grew to love about myself, it was all bred from pain. The most painful moments in my life, have been knitted together and each of them has molded me into the woman that I am today. This was an ironic observation because this painful realization that occurred during that very conversation marked the beginning of a whole different kind of self-inflicted pain that it has taken much of my life to get past. The things that I learned about myself during that time of reflection took me to the opposite end of the spectrum. Instead of being unpleasant as a means to keep loved ones at bay, I started to see how great it felt to help others and how wonderful it was to be a blessing in other people's lives.

This simplistic moment that should have been profound and positively effective actually created the person whom I affectionately call Doormat Brenda. I was almost completely selfless and truly believed that my joy came directly from being the catalyst to bring happiness to the lives of others, no matter the cost to myself. Everything was 'yes' no matter what the ask was. I began helping others to my detriment which felt good in the moment but would ultimately leave me depleted. I felt as though, if I gave the people that I loved my all, and they in turn gave me their all, then ultimately we would be satisfied in our dealings thereby leaving everyone happy. Unrealistic right? I had no clue what I was doing to myself until it was too late.

What I didn't consider is that we all have different versions of what we consider to be our 'all' and if we aren't careful, unrealistic expectations can be formed. We will definitely get more into that later, but for now let's just say that I went into overkill and ran myself ragged. I overextended myself in not only deeds, but in affection and interactions as well. It's no surprise that one incident brought it all to a head and made me realize that I had been going about all of this the wrong way.

One day as I prepared for work I got a buzz on my cell phone. Across the screen was displayed screenshots of messages between my husband and one of his coworkers. My husband and I had been having issues and it was no secret to anyone who knew him that he was a cheater. I had accepted and taken him back a multitude of times at this point which provided him an air of arrogance. By the time I received these messages, I was so over the merry-go-round that our marriage had become. I just tossed the phone in his lap and watched his face as he read them. He took a look at the phone, tossed it on the bed and continued to dress as if nothing had happened. He was caught again, but his nonchalance had me staring into an abyss of impending violence. I paused, took a breath and quietly asked him. "Why?"

"Why what?!" he asked completely annoyed.

"Why am I not good enough? Why aren't my feelings worthy of being considered? Why is it that I love you unconditionally, take care of you and forgive you time and time again only to be mistreated?"

The room went absolutely silent. I waited with bated breath for his response. The moments ticked by and just when I thought that he wouldn't answer, he jumped up. Rage was clear on his face as he stood so quickly that he almost fell. Then he stood over me, fists balled in frustration and began to shout. I sat encapsulated in fear just knowing that like many other times before, this would end in violence. Instead he began to shout so loudly, so close to my face that I could feel the spittle fly from his mouth. He was daring me to speak, move or even blink. And I knew that right now, in this moment, I had zero fight left. He raged,

"You think I care about all of that?! You think that just because you do what I ask I'm indebted to you? You think you can keep me on by buying me things? You think you own me? You can't change me? I never asked you to do none of that? Everything that you claim you do for me, you're doing for you to keep me owing you!"

I didn't dare say a word. His anger very literally sucked the air out of the room and I couldn't even breathe, let alone muster up enough air to speak. We had been here before and I knew what a rebuttal would bring. I simply cowered back until his anger abated and he stormed from the room. When he finally slammed the door, I finally began to breathe. And with each breath came a realization.

"Was everything that I did to please him for naught? Was I seeking love through debts owed to me for favors performed? Since this was the way that I governed most of my relationships, was it something that everyone thought about me? Is he right?"

Each breath became more and more difficult and before I knew it, I was in the throes of a full-fledged panic attack. An ineffectual self-analysis was taking place and I couldn't make it stop. Ineffectual in the moment simply because these were the ramblings of a trapped rat. Yes he was caught and would find a way to deflect, but that didn't make what he was saying any less true. My attempt at being selfless had now turned into just another fault that I developed in an attempt to solicit the type of love that I wanted receive thereby creating unrealistic expectations from the people around me. I needed time to figure this out. It took years longer than it should have for me to finally sort this all out.

What do you think about the concept of being selfless? Do you think it's something that can be implemented in a more healthy manner than I went about it? Is it something that you struggle with at all?

Brenda Colter

HER Beautiful Mind

Clearly my marriage was on a serious discord and ultimately my husband and I parted ways. There were a lot of things that had to be taken into consideration prior to my making that decision. Some were spiritual and others were more emotional and mental. I then embarked on a voyage to unravel all that I learned so that I could find myself and identify where I took the wrong turn.

Deeper retrospection helped me to realize that I needed balance. Everything in life is about balance and anything in excess can be a bad thing. Think about it. Our bodies need water to thrive but even having too much can cause hyponatremia also known as water intoxication. So apparently, too much of a good thing is still too much. And so began my trek to find balance.

While studying I came across an interview with Iyanla Vanzant where she explained that we need to be self-full. That interview changed my entire perception and made me want to dig more into the concept of wholeness. Conceptually it simply means that we have to fill our own cups before we can fill anyone else's. When it comes to our interactions with people we want our "cups" to run over which means that what is in the cup is for us and whatever spills out is then for others. This is a way to ensure that we complete the internal work that needs to be done prior to meeting the needs of others first which is completely out of order.

Now we have all heard that before but if you're anything like me, it's much easier said than done. As women we feel obligated, more often than not, to cover the people for whom we care. We think about the people, places and things in our world that are solely our responsibility. We have children, spouses, family, friends, work, businesses and a myriad of other duties and tasks that we need to be sure are taken care of, but who takes care of us. Far too often we underestimate the importance of self-care. Just consider the fact that if we aren't whole and complete, what do we really have to offer others. Self-care goes far beyond bubble baths there is an entire self-exploration that generally needs to take place in order to even identify what invigorates us.

Do you see the benefit in wholeness or do you feel as though caring for loved ones is the only way that you can feel whole? Do you think that is a healthy way to be? Do you know what fuels your soul? Do you understand what it means to be self-full and how it differs from being selfless? What are some things that you can do in order to fill your own cup from time to time?

Brenda Colter

HER Beautiful Mind

*"I went from stressed to blessed,
and the only thing I changed was my mind!"*

~ Kat Hoyer

3

Who's Driving Your Car?

When it comes to self-care and fueling the spirit, I believe that it's very important for everyone to have something to assist in the process. I learned fairly early on, and quite by accident, that one thing that works for me is driving. I don't mean carting my children to this event or another. I don't mean driving family and friends from one destination to the next for little to no payment. I don't mean a daily commute to and from work. I mean an aimless, destination-less, pointless drive to nowhere. I discovered this when my daughters were very young.

They were only ten and a half months apart, so raising them in the early years was like having twins. Their father and I were very young and he had no younger siblings to help raise as I did, so his effectiveness as a parent was mediocre at best which left me feeling like a single parent a lot of the time. I'm not saying I was supermom... just that I had more experience than he did. I remember one day both girls were crying incessantly and I just couldn't get them to stop, and I had read somewhere that taking them on a drive might calm them and put them to sleep. I couldn't think of anything less desirable than two screaming kids in a car, but I had exhausted all other ideas and I was desperate!

    I got the girls and my older son dressed, bagged up some snacks, filled the sippy cups, strapped them in their car seats, hopped into a family member's borrowed vehicle and we were off. The first 10 minutes were hard. The girls were screaming and clearly not feeling this impromptu family outing and my son was grouchy because I had awakened him up for this field trip. I simply cranked up the radio to drown out the noise and drove. Eventually they all passed out and there was silence. I actually shed a few tears just thankful that they were quiet.

    Initially I just drove a few miles, long enough for them to fall asleep and figured I would transport them from the car to the house and they would remain asleep, but as soon as I turned off the car and opened the door, they were back at it again. So I hopped back into the driver seat and hit the highway. After they calmed down and fell back asleep, the energy in the car began to shift. I lowered the volume on the radio and just let my mind wander. Before I knew it, I was an hour from home and more relaxed than ever. I exited the freeway, and reentered in the opposite direction. I was heading home with a much more peaceful mind than I had left with. And just that simply, I had identified a new, nontoxic way to cope. Since I had now identified driving as my means of peace, it was no coincidence that when a friend of mine introduced me to her STEER self-coaching model, I was hooked.

    STEER creator Kat Hoyer describes STEER as a form of neuro-hacking. She further explains that it isn't like the typical mindset training that fades after a period of short time. It actually teaches you to train your brain for permanent changes which creates massive results affecting every aspect of your life. One great thing about STEER is that it takes a practical everyday occurrence (driving) and uses anecdotal analogies and comparisons to help ingratiate the material into your mind. While STEER definitely requires hard work and perseverance, it has proven itself to be the missing link in my overall process. After hearing countless motivational speeches, reading an inordinate number of self-help books and studying God's Word for answers, STEER has been the "how" that literally guides me through the act of solving the issues and concerns that I identify and encounter on a regular basis.

Through HER Beautiful Mind(HBM), I have been able to utilize the STEER model as one of the key concepts in my overall business. From the HBM Church Emotional Assistance Program to The Transcendence Beyond Program which has the specific purpose of aiding women in overcoming the past, STEER has been invaluable. The destination is spiritual elevation. This involves taking the practicality of the STEER model, ingratiating it with the Word of God and presenting it in a way that guides us to not just expect our blessings but to do the internal, analytical and necessary work to achieve not only our desired outcomes but God's vision for our lives as well. This work requires a complete overhaul in our thought processes which is why we need STEER. When it comes to retraining our brains, there has been nothing that has worked better for me. I now feel comfortable being the driver of my own life and success. Before we get into exactly what it means to retrain your brain lets ponder a few things.

What do you do to ensure your own personal growth? What books have you read? What do you listen to? Have you taken any classes or workshops? How have they worked out for you? If you have never done any of those things, what are some reasons? Are you looking forward to learning more about retraining your brain? Why or why not?

Brenda Colter

HER Beautiful Mind

So usually this is when I'm met with disbelief regarding the effectiveness of retraining the brain, and I really can't blame anyone for their skepticism. If someone would have told me during my worst times that thinking more clearly would be so easy for me, I would not have believed them in the least. The first thing that I want to make clear is that STEERing is not about creating or fabricating positive thoughts, it's about recognizing the realistic ones. STEER is actually an acronym for Situation, Thought, Emotion, Execution, Result. This is akin to the order of operations in mathematics, only it was created to guide your thoughts with Emotional Wellness in mind. We use scientific facts to help explain what we mean by "realistic thoughts" and also to help clients better understand how our brains actually work. STEER was not just haphazardly orchestrated. Kat worked hard to meticulously create a proven method that combines cognitive behavioral therapy with dialectical behavioral therapy in a way that makes learning it much more practical. I of course can't get into the most intimate details of STEER, but I would like to offer some basic facts that we teach in the program. This information barely scratches the surface of the program, but it will give you a generalized idea of how and why it works.

One of the first and most important things to understand is what a thought actually is. A thought is simply a sentence in your mind. In and of itself, it holds no weight or impact. It is the manifestation of our thoughts that draws the inferences. The average person has up to 80,000 thoughts a day. Of those thoughts 80% are negative and 95% of the negative thoughts are repetitive. This point illustrates exactly what a task it can be to even become more aware of our thoughts, much less control them. So developing this sense of awareness regarding our thought processes is the first and a very key component in learning and implementing the STEER model.

Since retraining your brain is a progressive process that compounds one step upon the other, the next step digs a little deeper than identification and cognizance of our thoughts. It now becomes necessary to scrutinize them. This is where we apply our thoughts to the emotions that they create and the consequences that eventually befall us if we prove incapable of controlling them. It is in this step of the process that we take each component of STEER and use one to expound each upon the next creating a foundation of critical thinking. This critical thinking aids in the "shift."

The "shift" is where the magic happens when it comes to retraining the brain. It is in this step that the culmination of all that has been learned thus far comes to order because you learn how to use the link between the first part of the process (being stalled, stuck or stagnant) and progress into more productive thoughts and outcomes. Initially, this process is something that takes time and I recommend that you write on a sheet of paper or a journal to take notes. But in due course, it becomes a natural way to process thoughts similar to going from a manual to automatic gear shift when driving. Once a person reaches this point, it's safe to say that you have officially rewired your brain to think more realistically. Realistic thinking places you back into the driver's seat of your life. Once I finally had STEER down and it had become my way of life, I not only accepted Kat's offer to become her business partner; I also built my own programs around the STEER model.

To transcend means to rise above, go beyond or exceed preconceived limits. The Transcendence Beyond Program is the driving force behind HER Beautiful Mind. HER Beautiful Mind is my baby, my heart and my gift from God. After coming to a more emotionally stable place in life and realizing that it is truly possible to overcome my past, I realized that it is my mission to help women of all ages overcome issues of their past or anything else that can be keeping you bound. Using my experience of transcending beyond my past, I now help empower women to transcend beyond anything or any place that they could have ever imagined. Far too often our limiting thoughts and beliefs about ourselves, our past and others place constraints on our interactions that are not conducive to creating healthy and meaningful connections and relationships.

Combining this established and effective method with the Word of God has been a proven formula for success. I successfully take "just pray about it" to the next level by showing that faith without work is indeed dead, and also providing a blueprint for the work that needs to be done. Everyone's work will be different. The intensity and specifics of the work that has to be done will vary from person to person as will the results. It is a tough road to travel but it's always been my belief that nothing worth having has ever been born in comfort.

When I think about my greatest accomplishments, they were bred from painful experiences and tough lessons. It takes a special person to hold a proverbial mirror before themselves, realize that they don't necessarily like all that they see and then do the work to make the necessary changes. What helped me was not only using a spiritual mirror, but also developing the tools needed to change the image. When you make the decision to transcend, pain can only last so long before it manifests into magnificence. Through my growth and development, it became my mission to toss you the keys and place you back into the driver seat of your life to help you STEER your life. So I ask again; Who's driving your car?

*"I don't want to be at the mercy of my emotions.
I want to use them, to enjoy them,
and to dominate them."*

~ Oscar Wilde

4

Transforming Experiences

Emotions are the epicenter of our beings. Everything discussed thus far has explained how and why it is important that we retrain our brains to think more practically and logically throughout our lives. Now we can get into why it is important. All in all, we are creating a better version of ourselves, not just for ourselves but also to transform the experiences that we have with others. In today's society, so many of our day to day interactions with others leaves us feeling either wound up or completely numb. Learning how to govern our thoughts and emotions not only transcend us to new levels, it also helps us to understand the people who we love and with whom we associate much better. Strengthening relationships is also a key component to achieving peace in our own lives. What we have learned thus far in life should increase our emotional intelligence. The first question that I get when explaining this process is "What exactly is emotional intelligence?" My response is always the same; an internet search would land you many different definitions but ultimately it is the art of awareness, understanding and governance of ones emotions. Not just our emotions but those of others as well. You also may hear it referred to as EQ (emotional quotient) or EI (emotional intelligence) as well. Just as our IQ is based on applied knowledge in general, our EQ is the same as it relates to emotions. While there are no standardized tests to measure EQ, there are tests available that can give you a general idea of where you fall on the EQ scale. These quizzes also often offer methods to increase your capacity if you find yourself to be limited.

You may wonder what we have to gain from ensuring that we have a high EQ. I typically offer a myriad of reasons, but here we will just discuss a few. To begin, having a more firm understanding of our emotions creates a more likely ability to control them. If you're anything like me, there are times where you either do or have allowed your reactions to situations to be governed by raw emotion. Don't worry, in most cases we are not at fault due to a lack of information. We are however responsible for learning and controlling our thoughts and emotions once we know that the possibility is there. Unfortunately, we live in a culture where most of us have never been taught exactly how to control our thoughts and emotions, we were just told to do it. Well try telling a drowning person to swim if they've never learned how. That would be pretty difficult.

So let's get you just a tidbit of information that can assist you in understanding why impulsiveness and self-control may be a bit of an issue for you when you are feeling emotional. Our limbic system is the part of our brains that controls our thoughts, emotions and impulse. So that I don't bore you to sleep we will just say that our brains are wired so that the feeling region kicks in before the thinking region. If we don't learn control our feelings, this is what creates the reactions that are generally not healthy for us. I can actually remember one specific time prior to my learning to develop emotional intelligence that almost caused me some serious problems.

In traffic is where I find myself STEERing most often, no pun intended. I have no clue what it is about the road that makes folks irrational and (for lack of a better word) dumb. I'm using the word dumb in reference to my own actions that day more than anyone else's. On this particular day, I was in traffic heading home from work. As I approached an intersection, a car to my right in a turn only lane almost hits me trying to get over into my lane. I assume that the driver realized, too late, that they needed to be in the lane that I was occupying. We avoided a collision and ultimately the car ended up behind me. The light turns green and we are now on a one lane stretch of road. Now I am driving the speed limit, this fool is barreling down on my car, blowing his horn, flashing his lights and attempting to force me to drive faster.

During this encounter, I'm definitely screaming a few choice expletives and raising my fists in anger. This guy rode my bumper with this obnoxious behavior for about a mile and a half until he got to his turn, at which time he pulled next to me at the light, held up his middle finger and screamed in my direction a few choice, VERY colorful adjectives of his own. That was it! It was on! I took a sharp turn, followed him and mimicked his irresponsible and dangerous behavior (see why I called myself dumb earlier?). By this time he thinks I'm a nutcase and tries to out run me, but I was on him. I followed him to his destination, waited for him to stop and we had it out right then and there. A curse filled, screaming, disrespectful shouting match with a stranger who was easily 50 pounds heavier than I, he had a good foot or so on me in height and he was a man. I didn't care, I was running on unadulterated emotion; no thought whatsoever.

As I left the altercation, the reality of what had just happened hit me. Not only was this unintelligent, but a simple review of the possibilities and a pause to consider the possible consequences should have been enough to stop me from reacting the way that I did. In a same or similar situation today my reaction would be different and because this new way of thinking with my retrained brain is my normal now, it would only take a split second for me to analyze the situation totally differently. My increased EQ raises questions like: "Whoa, I wonder what's wrong that he's in such a hurry? I better let him go around." I don't know what that man could have had going on. Maybe he had just received a call about a family member's illness or death. Maybe he was late for work and is only allowed one more occurrence before he is fired. Maybe his pregnant wife is in labor and on her way to the hospital. The point is, increasing our EQ also increases our awareness of the fact that we have no clue what is going on in the day to day lives of others. It forces us to step outside ourselves and consider how others may be feeling while also forcing us to take an internal glimpse and see what we may be deflecting or reflecting. We can then use that information to communicate more effectively and understandingly.

Now you see why in my case learning about EI was imperative to not only my day to day interactions, but my survival even. Do you ever find yourself flying off the handle in situations that you later realize could have been handled differently. How do you handle that? Does it create issues in your life and relationships. If you have overcome this, what was the method that you used. Do you think that you need to brush up on your EQ?

HER Beautiful Mind

Now that I was at a point in my life where the concept of retraining my brain was no longer a foreign concept, the possibilities of what I could achieve felt endless. I always knew that we could learn new things but I never considered thoughts and emotions to be part of the learning curve. As a matter of fact, when my now business partner told me that it was possible, I was skeptical. I knew that she had done tons of research on the brain and that in creating the STEER model, ensuring scientific accuracy was very important to her. So we had a conversation where she took the time to clarify exactly how this was possible.

What I have been able to gather from Kat's explanation and in my own research, the neural pathways in our brain are pretty much like an information highway. Neural pathways carry information from one part of our brain to the other. Fairly recent scientific discoveries are realizing about the brain that neural pathways can be altered or changed. There are a multitude of reasons why this can happen, but the most notable reasons are trauma, chemical changes and as we learn new things. We can actually create new pathways by considering and practicing new thoughts. The best example that I have heard likens neural pathways to a river. As a river flows, it wears a groove in the earth creating a path for the water to flow. Learning new things would be like digging a trench and redirecting the river creating a new direction for the water to flow and building a dam to stop the water from flowing in the old direction. After a while, the old path will dry up and the new path will spring anew. This is why our new thoughts become our new normal.

One of my most notable feats in the process of retraining my brain was overcoming Monday's. I know that Monday is rough for most of us, but I absolutely detested Monday's. Beginning Sunday night, I would get down and behave as a petulant child sentenced to a month's grounding. I would snarl, growl or become just plain old melancholy in anticipation of Monday. As a result, I definitely created an energy around that day that caused negativity to befall me more often on that day than any other. I actually have journal entries to prove it. I now know that there were plenty of scientific and metaphysical happenings going on in my brain and my surroundings. From my reticular activating system to the weekly amygdala hijack to the law of attraction, I was training my brain to see nothing but negativity where Monday was concerned. I decided that this pattern would be the first that I would challenge on my road to self-discovery. I set out to see if I could train my brain to think more positively about Monday's thereby creating a more positive existence on that day for myself.

I began on the Sunday before. When I would feel my mind drift off into negativity, I would force myself to think of three good things about the next day. Exercising gratitude for the good instead of focusing on the bad is always a great method to combat negative thoughts. I also made sure that I did not speak the negativity into existence. I began to understand that thoughts are powerful but words can govern the atmosphere. We as humans are definitely not perfect so there were times when I slipped up out of habit. In that instance, I would implement disciplinary measures for myself such as no desert with dinner, or no soda the next day. Something simple but important to me and I solicited my children to hold me accountable.

On Monday, I would begin the day with my normal prayer and bible reading, but I also added a positive affirmation. Every day I would look in the mirror and say "Today is Monday and I thank God for waking me up. Today will be an amazing day and there is no reason that it should be any less amazing than any other day. Today I will excel." Ultimately, my dread for Monday's subsided and I ceased to experience the overwhelming dread on

Sunday's as well. I'm not vapid enough to believe that saying the mantra or the Sunday discipline system worked in and of themselves. However; they made me more mindful of my behaviors which I am sure affected others around me and created a more positive energy surrounding me. I no longer need the affirmation. Monday now is just like any other day of the week.

Is there a situation in your life in which you consistently struggle. Have you ever tried positive affirmations or a reward/discipline system? Do you believe that it is possible to retrain your brain. What do you think your next step will be?

Brenda Colter

HER Beautiful Mind

When someone asks me what I do, and I reply that I am an Emotional Wellness Enthusiast it usually garners a look of sheer confusion. I'm always amazed at the way society places such a stringent focus on physical wellness yet treats our emotional and mental health as though they are an afterthought. In reality, each part of our beings whether it be spiritual, mental, physical or emotional require a specific balance in order for us to function at our full capacity. So just as we strive to beware of what we eat, drink or consume in order to maintain physical wellness we should also take the time to ensure Emotional Wellness.

After taking what you have learned so far about emotional intelligence and using that to retrain the brain, brings us to the point of maintenance. After a diet you have to work to maintain your newfound weight loss. When you have your body looking the way that you want you have to continue a workout regimen to ensure that you stay nice and tight. The same is to be said about Emotional Wellness. Through mindful stress relief, self-care and the development of inner strength, we can develop an Emotional Wellness regimen that works for you and also find yourself on the path to positive energy and eventually a more powerful you.

Once you have done the work to achieve the level of peace that you aspire to have, it takes work to maintain it. It is this area where we see the most relapse so I am always careful to be very clear on this matter. STEER is what we call a self-coaching model. That simply means that the ultimate goal is to get to where you can redirect your thoughts on your own; however there is still an entire community created for those moments when you find yourself spinning out. We are only human, after all. Since at this point, there is no magic pill to make everything better, the best thing to do is to accept the tools that work for you and utilize them in your day to day life.

In achieving a firmer grip on your own thoughts and emotions, you are then prepared to utilize what you have learned to build and grow the relationships with the people for whom you care. It is through a journey of self-exploration that you learn to be the driver of your own emotions and arrive at a destination of understanding, an understanding of not only yourself, but of others as well.

What do you think about Emotional Wellness as a necessary tool for peaceful survival? Did you know about it before? Does this change what you previously thought? What are some things that you can do to begin your journey toward positivity?

HER Beautiful Mind

"Caring enough to learn a person's love language could be the key to unlocking their soul."

~ Brenda Colter

5

Building Realistic Relationships

The Five Love Languages is a book by Gary Chapman that rocked me to my core when while reading it, I realized that finding or expressing love may not be my issue. My issue may actually be that I don't understand or respect the way that different people choose to display their love. This is the key to ensuring that your relationships and interactions with others is based on factual information and a proven track record rather than our own desires. This is the beginning of a realistic relationship rather than the illusion that we often have in our minds of what an interaction should entail.

There are so many fear inducing aspects of love. Not just romantic love, but any relational association where our hearts and emotions can be negatively affected in any way. Of all of those fears, I have found that loving someone more than they do us seems to be by far one of the most difficult to experience. It takes a distinct degree of self-assuredness to remain secure in a relationship where you felt as though your emotional output was always greater than that which you received. In these cases, it's important to know and acknowledge the Love Languages of the parties involved. Once we learn a person's love language, we will likely find that just because they love us differently than we love them, does not mean that they love us any less than we love them. Love is all about expression. Developing lasting relationships with others means that we are prepared to take their need for love and appreciation seriously and learn to speak their love language.

Jada Pinkett-Smith once said that "Every person we will ever meet is brokenhearted. I realized that people don't break my heart, it is my false beliefs around love and my unrealistic expectations of people that break my heart." It took hard work and dedication to wrap my mind around what she was saying. The primitive "pre-STEER" part of my brain wanted to dismiss her words all together. After all, how can I be blamed for what another person chose to do to me? How can I be to blame for the selfish way that someone else acted, in effect, causing my heart to become shattered into a million pieces. Forget that! It was their fault and their fault only! I would not be held responsible for their actions! After I got out of my feelings, I considered my former marriage and through my developed EQ, I was able to eventually shift my thoughts about it.

When I met my ex-husband, it was his sad eyes that drew me to him. His quiet melancholy demeanor intrigued me. He always seemed to be deep in thought, thinking up a master plan and it didn't help that he was definitely not hard on the eyes. We became fast friends in our crew. There were about 10 or so of us that would hang out on a regular basis and it began to become a familiar sight to see us ducked off in a corner talking in the midst of the chaos that was usually going on around us. We took those days to get to know one another. I told him of my brokenness. He learned things about my past that no one ever knew and I still haven't decided if anyone else ever will. He told me things about his past that made my heart physically ache for him.

The day that we decided we wanted to be together he gave me a warning that would give an emotionally well and sensible person pause. He told me that because of his past, it was hard for him to express his love in a normal way. He told me that I would need to teach him how to love in general and I especially needed to teach him how I needed to be loved. This is what eventually broke us apart. His lack of knowledge of himself created an insecurity that could never be quelled by anything besides a deeper exploration of his own past. It was not something that I could teach or show him. I know that now, but back then I thought I could love him into loving himself and me.

What I learned in reviewing this as the beginning of the relationship that led to marriage is that I should have taken a pause for the cause in that moment. The subsequent pain that I endured during that relationship was of my own volition because I expected something that he clearly did not have the ability to give. There was nothing about him that changed or developed that could have altered that reality. I learned then that our expectations of others should align with what they show us. It's not fair of us to expect anything more than what they show us that they can give. Developing unrealistic expectations is a real relationship killer. It's imperative that we protect ourselves from ourselves where this is concerned.

Can you think of a relationship or situation where your judgement was impaired and in hindsight you realize that you could have endured less pain had you considered the truth? Have you ever pulled the wool over your own eyes and as a result had to redirect your path? How did you get back on track? Were there specific methods that you followed? Do you agree that through the adjustment of expectations we can form more powerful relationships with the people in our lives?

Brenda Colter

Once I realized that I could take such a significant relationship failure and learn from it, I decided that it would behoove me to analyze any interactions from which I still remained hurt or damaged. As I began to pick each relationship apart, I was able to identify the error in my ways and what I could do to ensure that I did not continue to repeat my personal errors. The most valuable lesson that STEER helped me to learn is that even in dual party interactions, the only person for whom I am responsible or can control is myself.

It is my responsibility to govern my behavior in a way that honors me, exemplifies who I want to be in Christ and in the interest of universal influence, places me in a position to win. I needed to become more mindful of the energy that I was creating when I made decisions. I was on a journey and the first stop was repairing (my end) of the broken relationships in my life and now that I had done the work, I had a surefire process.

Now that I had done the self-exploration and introspection, I felt capable to review my interactions with others. The first step was acknowledgement. I had to acknowledge that I had created unrealistic expectations of almost everyone who I had alienated in any way. It was purely unintentional and it was also unfair. In my eyes, relationships are governed best when each party practices the law of reciprocity. The law of reciprocity is a basic law of human nature where what one gives, one receives. This can include energy, behavior, deed and a whole host of interactions. Where the rule gets twisted is at the intent of the giver. In my case, I'm a giver because it makes me feel good to give and I hope that I am creating a relationship built on reciprocity, not out of obligation but out of appreciation and gratitude. What I never realized is that some would see this as a form of manipulation.

I can never forget a time where this was more prevalent than ever. My relationship with one of my ex's was a tumultuous one. We're great friends and can co-parent like nobody's business now, but we were very young when we dated. Both of us were too young and too damaged to even be attempting "playing house" like we were doing so there was always contention and frustration between us. I was learning how to navigate being a mother at a very young age and he was becoming a man in the only way that he knew how. He was routinely unfaithful and just plain old messy for lack of a better term.

Being young and immature, I decided that the only way that he would see the error in his ways would be for me to offer him a dose of his own medicine. I began to see another guy on the side, someone we both knew. Our town is fairly small so I knew that it would only be a matter of time before he found out. Sure enough, I had this guy over and there was a bang on the door. Just from the cadence of the knock, I knew exactly who it was. I took my time getting to the door and when I did, he came bursting in like a hurricane. He was livid and in rare form. How could I betray him like this? Why this guy? Couldn't I have been more careful? Didn't I care how much I was hurting him? I did, but I couldn't let him know it.

In the end, the other guy left and my ex and I sat down to have a conversation. In this conversation he explained that he couldn't be with me anymore. Yes, you read that right. HE couldn't be with ME! This man whom I had forgiven countless times. This man who had broken my heart time and time again. This man who maintained a totally separate relationship with another woman because I felt it was easier to allow it than to fight it, was telling me that my betrayal ran too deep for him to forgive. I was flabbergasted. With tears in my eyes I looked at him and asked,

"After all of these times that I have forgiven you, after all of the chances that I gave you, after all that I've done for you, you're telling me that you're leaving me?"

He looked back at me dead in my eyes and as cool as a cucumber and said, "I never asked you to do any of that. You did that on your own because that's what you wanted to do. That doesn't mean that I have to do it." And with that closing remark, he left.

It's amazing how in hindsight I can see each instance of my life where this lesson played over and over in an attempt to get me to learn it. That's something we don't realize. Everything that happens in our lives is for a reason. There is some lesson in it, and if we don't learn it that lesson will repeat itself over and over again until we get it.

Do you agree that our interactions with others should contain the law of reciprocity? Can you think of any instances where you have unrealistic expectations of others that may need to be adjusted? Is there a level of acceptance that you have to reach when it comes to the character of the people who you love?

HER Beautiful Mind

Acknowledgement and acceptance had now provided me with the peace and direction that I needed to mend the broken relationships and also build new, more healthy and realistic ones. I remember reading a quote that said something to the effect of "You know that you're strong when you have to forgive someone who isn't sorry," this concept was the first test of my newfound acknowledgement and acceptance of others.

I realized very early on in my personal growth process that not everyone will grow at the rate that we would like for them to. Where I saw broken relationships as mutually dismantled, most people while willing to accept my apologies, had no intentions on accepting any kind of wrongdoing whatsoever. I made the very tough decision to forgive them anyway. I also want to offer a disclaimer by explaining that forgiving these people did not mean that I necessarily allowed them back into my life in the capacity that they were previously. It simply meant that I harbored no ill will in my heart for them and wanted to be sure that they were aware of that.

As I began to navigate through the broken shards of my interactions with others, something amazing happened. I realized that my connections and interactions were more authentic. I still ran across people that I may not have particularly liked or wanted to be around, but I developed a respect for everyone that I encountered. I respected them, because I respected the emotional and/or mental place that they may have been in life. I realized that it is perfectly okay that we all grow and change at different rates and in different areas of our lives. God made us all unique unto ourselves for a specific reason and it is not my business or responsibility to attempt to decipher another person's reason. Once I stopped manipulating relationships to morph into whatever it is that I envisioned them to be, I was left with the blessing of just being able to enjoy them.

There is a tribe of people who believe that little to no expectations are the key to happiness. They believe that if we have low or no expectations of others, then we can't be disappointed. I do not want my viewpoint to be confused with that belief. I actually consider that to be a form of pessimism that can draw negative energy. No, what I am saying is that we need to use a person's behavior to realistically set our expectations so that we never expect more than they have previously displayed that they are able or willing to offer. What I am talking about is realism.

Are there some things that you can do to develop a better or more productive understanding of your relational interactions? Are there some changes that you can make in your viewpoint to help guide your relationships to a more realistic place? In your life, with whom will you begin?

HER Beautiful Mind

"My highest ambition is to crawl out from under the ash and laugh at all the things that thought they could bury me"

~ Rudy Francisco

6

Positive Energy = Powerful you

As I reflected on all of the most pertinent lessons that I have learned in the process of developing myself into the woman that I know God intends for me to be, the first notable thing is that I am forever a work in progress. I don't mean that as an excuse, but it definitely keeps me humble on the path and ensures that I will continue to take a look at what I can do to remedy the issues in my life and the role that I play in the situations that may turn out to be less than stellar. I realize that sometimes we can be our own worst enemies.

One of the most difficult things in this world to do is to accept our own mistakes and errors of our ways. It's hard to look inside yourself only to see something distasteful staring back. It's especially hard when this reflection caused you to lose or miss out on something or someone that you hold dear. It would befit us all to develop the ability to see this as an opportunity for growth. Examining deep within ourselves allows us to learn and expand our thought processes. Being as organic and genuine as possible ensures an inner peace that can't be matched. I'm learning daily to be more open and honest. It is certainly not easy because I don't like to be vulnerable, but it is necessary to progress through each chapter in my life.

Extract the positive in each situation that you face by realizing that missed opportunities are simply learning experiences that we need to use to move forward and gain wisdom. We cannot change a troubled yesterday, but we can harness the energy that remains to mold a better tomorrow. Being bitter and lashing out as a result of your own self-inflicted pain and frustration only hurts us in the long run. Growing angry at a person for getting tired of our shenanigans or becoming upset with another person who finds value in what we took for granted is counterproductive and a complete waste of energy that could be better utilized if it were focused in a more positive direction. Move on, find happiness and learn from the pain. Anything else could prove to be mentally, emotionally and possibly physically dangerous.

Life is way too short to keep our thoughts and feelings bottled in. Most of us find it very hard to communicate due to fear of rejection and inadequacy. Finding peace in removing unwarranted expectations of others from the forefront of our concerns can help immensely. That way, our expressions are simply expressions and not solicitations for reciprocity. Accept that not everyone thinks or feels the way that you do, and that's okay. Happiness is internal and if you do it right it's eternal. It feels great that now instead of people constantly asking me what is wrong, I more frequently am asked how I remain optimistic during trials or adversity. My initial reply is don't get it twisted, I have my moments when negativity kicks up and rears its ugly head. I get sad, I get angry, I get melancholy, I get frustrated. I just don't dwell on it. My goal in life is to find the lesson in EVERYTHING and since knowledge is power, I end up stronger. The point is, we all fall but getting up is the true determination of strength.

In building strength it's important to understand where the most complex difficulties lie. I believe that perhaps of all the lessons that we learn while on this earth, the toughest ones are about love. Most of us spend our lives waiting, hoping, praying, preparing and dreaming about love. Whether it's the love of a mate, spouse, significant other, friend or family member. We all have or will encounter something confusing, painful, irritating, or even debilitating about love. Ultimately, the answers are generally found in understanding, expectations, communication and trust (or lack of each of these things). It's also very important to remember that sometimes love and strength come from a source far beyond our realm of capabilities or comprehension.

Constantly through the years, I have also made it a priority to strengthen my relationship with God. That in and of itself is the key to my survival. I once had a conversation with a friend who insists that God doesn't hear him. This prompted a discussion about the fact that God is not a genie to grant your every wish. He's a parent to do what's best for you even when YOU don't know what that is. He is all seeing, He is all knowing and He is all loving. He IS the I Am, and I can promise that if your line of communication with God is cut, you can bet your bottom dollar that the disconnect occurred on your end. But all is never lost. He's waiting for you to seek Him through prayer and walking in His light. Prayer is the catalyst that forms a two way communication, and your spiritual walk let's him know that you are willing to do His work. Prayer is our protection, our ordained weapon used to fight the good fight. When you speak to Him, seal your prayer in Jesus' name and let the Holy Spirit carry your message and hand deliver it personally. He WILL speak back. You just need to be open and ready to listen to Him.

The road to peace, love and power is usually full of potholes. But if we choose to learn from our mistakes and STEER toward a more positive outcome, the reward should outweigh the risk. Life is for living and peace isn't just for the dead and buried! Allowing negative energy and people to drive us off into a ditch could be detrimental to our growth process. Ultimately, you have to take the good with the bad and keep your eyes on the road. Learn, grow, laugh, love and when you don't know what else to do... STEER.

Now that I've yammered on incessantly for the last six chapters, you may wonder what the point is. What is it that I want you to walk away with? I want you to walk away in peace, love and power. I want you to walk way ready, willing and understanding what it will take to improve your relational acumen. We all have some sort of internal demons that we fight daily. Some are more prevalent than others. If we don't begin a regimen of positivity, reflection, meditation and prayer it can become very difficult to see the light at the end of the tunnel. Believe that the things you feel will become the enemy's plan of attack if we don't take the time to separate what we feel from reality. I want you to utilize all of your findings during your reflection on the topics that we reviewed here to realize a more powerful, beautiful and mindful you.

What have you learned throughout this process? In reading, do you think there are changes that you need to implement in your day to day life and interactions? Are the changes that you now know that you need to make, different from what you thought them to be when you first began? Where do you want your next steps to lead you? What do you believe those steps need to be?

Life is a series of events and occurrences that shape and mold our futures into our destiny. There will definitely be glitches along the way. You'll mess up, you'll shatter and be forced to pray for the strength to put yourself together again. The trick is to take ALL of these occurrences and mold them into knowledge and wisdom, which both breed growth. Stand tall, stay strong and WHEN you slip (because we all do) collect yourself, straighten your crown and keep it moving... like a Boss!

Brenda Colter

Claim Your Free Gift!

From Trying to Triumphant: A 21 Day Challenge To Overcoming is designed for growth and personal development. This 21 challenge dares you to defy self-depreciating mindsets and limiting beliefs that keep us feeling bound and will propel you into purpose. This challenge will help you to:

- Embark on a journey to self-awareness
- Learn the importance of self-acceptance
- Begin to implement the practice of self-love

Each of these are key stops on the road to becoming a more powerful, beautiful, mindful you!

How: Go to www.herbeautifulmind220.com and click on HBM Shop click on the challenge and at checkout put in this code: HBMOVRCM to claim this free gift

About The Author

Brenda Colter is a proud native of Akron, Ohio. As an Emotional Wellness Coach Brenda merges her roles as coach, mentor, author and public speaker with the Word of God to empower others to overcome their past by teaching mindfulness and thought management in a way that makes it clear and practical. She currently functions as the owner of HER Beautiful Mind, founder of BeTheReason and the Vice President of SYLC Consulting. As a teen mother and high school drop-out, Brenda worked hard to overcome the mistakes and misfortunes of her past to climb the corporate ladder of a Fortune 500 company before realizing that God had a much larger calling on her life. Determined to utilize the story of her life as an empowerment tool for others, Brenda studied, prayed and ultimately completed her coaching certification. Resolute in her calling to become a stellar life and business coach, Brenda created the *HBM Church Emotional Assistance Program* and *The Transcendence Beyond Program*.

As a divorced mother of four and a grandmother, Brenda's mission is to always show the world that no matter where you've come from, no matter how you've been burned, it's always possible to rise up from the ashes and begin anew. It is her core belief that "Pain only lasts so long before it manifests into magnificence."

www.ingramcontent.com/pod-product-compliance
Lightning Source LLC
Chambersburg PA
CBHW062028290426
44108CB00025B/2818